WE THE PEOPLE

The Ojibwe
and Their History

by Natalie M. Rosinsky

Content Adviser: Bruce Bernstein, Ph.D.,
Assistant Director for Cultural Resources,
National Museum of the American Indian, Smithsonian Institution

Reading Adviser: Rosemary G. Palmer, Ph.D.,
Department of Literacy, College of Education,
Boise State University

COMPASS POINT BOOKS
MINNEAPOLIS, MINNESOTA

Compass Point Books
3109 West 50th Street, #115
Minneapolis, MN 55410

Visit Compass Point Books on the Internet at www.compasspointbooks.com
or e-mail your request to custserv@compasspointbooks.com

On the cover: A detail from an 1857 painting by Seth Eastman
of Ojibwe women gathering wild rice

Photographs ©: Stock Montage, cover; Prints Old and Rare, back cover (far left), 15, 32; Library of Congress, back cover, 8, 16; Layne Kennedy/Corbis, 4; Hampden Maps/Michael Bruff, 5; Minnesota Historical Society/ Henry Lewis, 6; Lowell Georgia/Corbis, 9; Peter Beck/Corbis, 10; Marilyn "Angel" Wynn, 12, 23, 24; Courtesy W. Duncan and Nivin MacMillan and Afton Historical Society Press, 13; Minnesota Historical Society, 14, 34; MPI/Getty Images, 17, 19, 30; Images reprinted by the courtesy of the Great Lakes Indian Fish & Wildlife Commission, Odanah, WI, 20, 39; Bruce Coleman, Inc./Wayne Lankinen, 21; Minnesota Historical Society/ Fanny Corbaux, 22; Werner Forman/Corbis, 25; Mary Evans Picture Library, 26; Hulton Archive/Getty Images, 28; Hulton-Deutsch Collection/Corbis, 29; Minnesota Historical Society/Matthew B. Brady, 31; Minnesota Historical Society/Charles Alfred Zimmerman, 33; Bettmann/Corbis, 36; Ed Kashi/Corbis, 37; Keri Pickett/Time Life Pictures/Getty Images, 38; Kit Breen, 40; Phil Schermeister/Corbis, 41.

Creative Director: Terri Foley
Managing Editor: Catherine Neitge
Art Director: Keith Griffin
Photo Researcher: Marcie C. Spence
Designer/Page production: Bradfordesign, Inc./Bobbie Nuytten
Cartographer: XNR Productions, Inc.

Library of Congress Cataloging-in-Publication Data
Rosinsky, Natalie M. (Natalie Myra)
  The Ojibwe and their history / by Natalie M. Rosinsky.
      p. cm—(We the people)
  Includes bibliographical references and index.
  ISBN 0-7565-0843-6 (hardcover)
  1. Ojibwe Indians—History—Juvenile literature. 2. Ojibwe Indians—Social life and customs—Juvenile literature. I. Title. II. We the people (Series) (Compass Point Books)
  JK5116.B42 2005
  977.004'97333-dc22   2004018965

TABLE OF CONTENTS

A DEATH MARCH

It was December 1850—that bitterly cold time of year the Ojibwe people call Small Spirits Moon. Several thousand Ojibwe were gathered in Sandy Lake, in what is now northern Minnesota. More than a foot of snow lay on the ground. Despite these terrible conditions, many Ojibwe set

The winters are cold and snowy in northern Minnesota.

A 1790 engraving of an Ojibwe family

out on a long journey home. Sandy Lake was not where they lived, and they did not want to be there. They wanted to go back home—but that was a long ways away in Wisconsin and Michigan.

It was trickery and false promises that had brought them to faraway Sandy Lake in this dangerous winter season. The Ojibwe had already signed many treaties with the government of the United States. These treaties gave American settlers the use of some Ojibwe land in exchange for money and supplies. Some government officials, though, wanted the Ojibwe to leave their traditional lands. These officials purposefully sent food and other supplies that had been promised to the Ojibwe to distant Sandy Lake.

Only in October 1850, during Falling Leaves Moon, had the Ojibwe learned the location of their promised supplies. To reach these quickly, they traveled with little winter equipment. Yet, when the Ojibwe

This wood engraving of Sandy Lake was published in a London newspaper in 1858.

arrived at Sandy Lake, the supplies were not there. None arrived in November either, the time of the Freezing Moon. More than 150 Ojibwe died from hunger and diseases such as measles as they waited.

When food, much of it rotten, finally came in early December, even the strongest warriors were suffering. One Indian agent wrote about the government's plan "to throw every obstacle in the way of [the Ojibwe] returning to their old homes."

Nearly 250 more Ojibwe died as they painfully made their way homeward on what came to be called the Wisconsin Death March. Before they even set out, they were weak with hunger. Some were sick. Many did not even have the rolls of birch bark, woven mats, or fur hides that were typically used to keep their winter wigwams warm. Because they came from different tribes in Wisconsin and upper Michigan, some Ojibwe would have to travel 285 miles (456 kilometers) on foot to reach their loved ones. Others, if they survived, would have to travel more than 400 miles

(640 km). Yet, even though they knew they might die along the way, these desperate people were determined to reach their homes.

Chief Hole-in-the-Day later described Sandy Lake as a "grave-yard" for his people.

Many years before, though, the Ojibwe had made an even longer journey. That trip stemmed from their own strong beliefs and connections with the earth.

Chief Hole-in-the-Day in about 1864

WHO ARE THE OJIBWE?

The ancestors of the Ojibwe lived on the Eastern seaboard. About the year 900, they began to move slowly westward. The Ojibwe traveled and were allies with two other native peoples, the Ottawa and the Potawatomi. These close allies were known as the Council of the Three Fires. Ojibwe leaders had decided to follow a prophecy. It said their people would find happiness in the West, in a place where food grew on water. Between 1400 and 1545, the Ojibwe reached the Midwest. They recognized this area as their destination because food—wild rice—grew in the lakes there.

Wild rice grows in a lake in Minnesota.

9

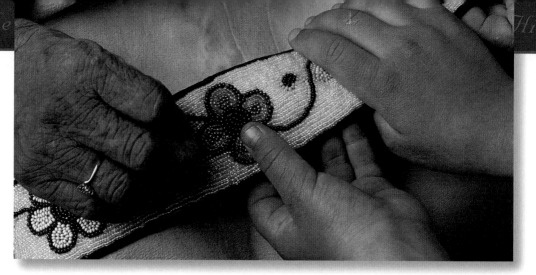

An elderly woman shares Ojibwe traditions with a child.

The Ojibwe settled across a wide area that today includes the states of North Dakota and Montana, and the Canadian provinces of Ontario, Manitoba, and Saskatchewan. While the western people share their history and some traditions, it is the Ojibwe of Michigan, Wisconsin, and Minnesota who have kept most of their original woodlands traditions. Today, about 80,000 Ojibwe live in these three Midwestern states bordering the Great Lakes. More than half of these Ojibwe live on reservations located there.

The Ojibwe are also known as the Chippewa. This name may have come from European traders not hearing or saying "Ojibwe" correctly. The Ojibwe prefer the name Ojibwe rather than Chippewa. In their own language, they call themselves and other native peoples the Anishinabe, which means "original people." The Ojibwe speak Ojibemowin, which is one language in the large family of Algonquian languages.

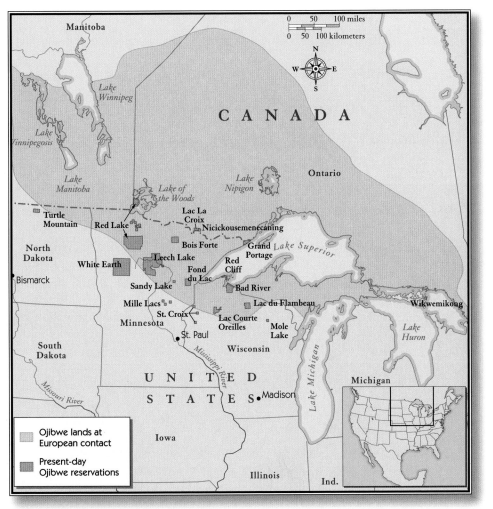

Ojibwe reservations are located in the United States and Canada.

FOLLOWING THE SEASONS

An Ojibwe elder, Night Flying Woman, remembers her grandmother telling her that their people's "life cycle follows the circle designed by Mother Earth." As the seasons change, Ojibwe traditionally moved from place to place within their woodland territory. They set up homes close to the food sources available each season. Yet the Ojibwe were not full nomads. They returned to the same

Canadian artist Paul Kane painted this Ojibwe village in 1846.

places each year. Often, Ojibwe would rebuild homes on frameworks they had left behind.

In the early spring, Ojibwe camped at their sugar-making location. There, they tapped maple trees for their sweet sap. They boiled this into syrup and sugar that flavored foods. During these weeks, the Ojibwe lived in round or cone-shaped wigwams with hardwood frames. Each year, the Ojibwe covered these frames with fresh reeds or birch bark.

Artist Seth Eastman painted this Indian sugar camp in 1850.

13

An Ojibwe family and their canoe in 1900

In late spring and summer, Ojibwe moved to their camp near one of the area's many lakes or streams. Men fished with nets or spears carried in birch bark canoes. Sometimes they also hunted deer, moose, and birds. Families planted potatoes, corn, beans, and squash. Women and girls also gathered wild berries and plants for medicine. Some of this food, along with dried fish and meat, was stored underground for later use. Birch bark covered summer wigwams.

In the fall, Ojibwe moved to their wild rice camp near marshes. They gathered this food of their prophecy, which they called *mahnomin*. They knocked the rice into their canoes with long sticks. Later, they roasted and stored it. At this colder time, they lived in wigwams covered with animal skins.

During the bitter winter, Ojibwe men hunted and trapped beaver, moose, deer, bear, and rabbit. They fished through holes cut into ice-covered lakes. Ojibwe also ate the food they had stored. Larger wigwams in these colder months often held two campfires. The wigwams were covered with furs as well as skins.

In the mid-1800s, an Ojibwe woman named Nodinens described how her people would prepare for these seasonal moves. Like her father, many of them made their own calendars out of sticks. "He had a stick ᐅ long enough to last a year," she said, "and he always began a new stick in the fall. He cut a big notch for the first day of the new moon and a small notch for each of the other days."

The Ojibwe speared fish through holes in the ice.

"The Patterns of Life"

Parents, children, and sometimes grandparents lived together in a wigwam. In winter, this family traveled alone or perhaps with another, related family. This way, many hunters did not compete for food. Several families joined together for sugar making and harvesting wild rice. In summer, Ojibwe enjoyed gathering in larger camps of 300 to 400 people. They traded and celebrated. Couples married then. By tradition, the newlyweds were told, "You will share the same fire. You will walk the same trail."

An Ojibwe wedding ceremony

Women cooked. They made containers of birch bark and cedar. Sometimes they used their teeth to bite designs into these objects. Women prepared reed mats or furs for

Seth Eastman painted an Indian woman dressing a deerskin.

bedding and sewed animal skins into clothing and moccasins. Traditionally, Ojibwe women wore hide dresses. They added leggings and fur capes in cold weather. Men wore short leather clothes around the middle of their bodies called breechcloths. In cold weather, they added leather leggings, shirts, and capes. Women decorated clothing with dyed porcupine quills and beads in lovely flower patterns. Young girls were often proud to learn these skills.

Men made bows, arrows, snares, spears, and hoes. They used wood, stone, and animal bones for these tools. They crafted snowshoes and toboggans for winter transportation. Men built the birch bark canoes that they used to fish and gather rice. Boys felt grown up because learning these jobs meant they were becoming men.

Ojibwe babies were kept snug inside cradleboards. Ojibwe tucked moss around the babies' bottoms to keep them dry. Older children played with dolls or toy bows and arrows. They played hide and seek and running and wrestling games. Ojibwe enjoyed telling and listening to

An 1826 painting of an Ojibwe woman and her baby

stories. Through stories, grandparents and other elders often taught children Ojibwe values and beliefs. These included sharing, honesty, and treating all living things with respect. As Night Flying Woman's grandmother said to her when she was a little girl, "Listen, and you will hear the patterns of life."

After their marriage, young couples lived at first with the bride's family, but children belonged to a father's clan. Membership in a clan was important. All members of a clan were supposed to help one another. The original Ojibwe clans were named for the crane, bear, marten, fish,

The Great Lakes Indian Fish and Wildlife's 2004 annual poster features the lynx. Called bizhiw *in Ojibwe, it is an important clan symbol.*

loon, deer, and bird. Ojibwe believed that people had some qualities of their clan creature. A member of the deer clan named L'Anse joyfully said, "The deer is my companion; I follow his life. I never need a compass to go through the woods, for I am able to find my way just like a deer."

Sometimes, though, clan membership could involve less positive qualities.

According to William Warren, an early historian of the Ojibwe, a member of the bear clan was often as "ill-tempered and fond of fighting" as that animal—and that member had a bearlike "long, thick, coarse head of blackest hair," too.

People born into the bear clan are protectors of the community, along with the lynx and wolf clans.

"THE POWER OF THE EARTH"

Ojibwe believed that the world was created by one great spirit, which they called Gitchi Manitou. They believed that all living creatures and parts of Earth had their own sacred spirits, too. They called plants and animals their "brothers." Before gathering food and when hunting, Ojibwe offered thanks to the spirit of the land or animal.

An 1840 engraving of the Ojibwe

Sacred tobacco is kept in a beaded pouch.

Leaving some tobacco was often part of this thanks. Ojibwe consider tobacco a sacred plant. Their prayers to Gitchi Manitou included smoking tobacco in a special, decorated pipe. They also burned other sacred plants such as sage, sweetgrass, and cedar. Prayers might be spoken, sung, or danced.

Some ceremonies took place in special houses called sweat lodges. Sometimes, Ojibwe fasted to gain knowledge about the spirit world. Before becoming adults, Ojibwe boys and girls went through different ceremonies that included fasting. Boys discovered their personal spirits, or manitous, and paths in life. Girls learned the special duties of mothers.

Ojibwe believed that dreams were also connections to the spirit world. As Night Flying Woman's grandmother said, "In dreams [Gitchi Manitou] gives the power of the Earth to the Ojibwe." Children learned to remember and interpret their dreams. Sometimes, Ojibwe made and hung special webs called dream catchers. These were said to prevent bad dreams from reaching people.

A dream catcher at sunset

24

The Ojibwe were one of the few native peoples who wrote down their beliefs. They drew pictographs on birch bark scrolls. Healers who had special knowledge of plants and the spirit world kept the scrolls safe. These respected men and women were called the Midewiwin.

Ojibwe pictographs were drawn on birch bark.

CHANGE AND LOSS

A council of Ojibwe leaders met in the summer. They made decisions involving all Ojibwe, such as agreements with other nations. Each clan sent a member who knew about the decisions to be made. Respected healers might also be sent. This council talked about problems until its members agreed.

An initiation ceremony was held for respected healers.

Many new problems began for the Ojibwe in the early 1600s, when French explorers and fur traders reached their territory. Explorer Samuel de Champlain was so impressed by the way birch bark canoes outran his heavier boats that he ordered his men to learn to make these canoes.

Yet European crafts and tools had a greater and, in many ways, harmful effect on the Ojibwe and other native peoples. They grew used to using the metal tools, guns, and cloth that the French traded them for beaver and other furs. Native peoples hunted and trapped so many animals, particularly beaver, that some became scarce. The neighboring Iroquois became eager for more hunting and trapping land. They conquered the Ojibwe and took some of their territory. Ojibwe then battled other neighboring peoples, the Dakota and the Fox, and took their land. Many Ojibwe warriors and others died in these wars.

Traders and Christian missionaries also brought terrible diseases such as smallpox with them. Because the Ojibwe had no immunity to these illnesses, many people

The Ojibwe battled other tribes from their canoes on Lake Superior.

died. Some Ojibwe who became Christian moved away from Ojibwe who had not.

Between 1754 and 1763, France and England fought to control the land and trade in North America. This was called the French and Indian War. The Ojibwe were allies of France. Their longtime enemies, the Iroquois, were allies of England. When England won, Ojibwe lost territory. England then controlled the fur trade.

When the American colonies fought England for their independence (1775–1783), the Ojibwe were again on the wrong side. They were allies of England during this Revolutionary War, but the Americans won. Ojibwe again lost territory. They suffered deaths in battle and from disease.

A 19th-century illustration of an Ojibwe war dance

"BUSINESS IN THE DARK CORNER"

Between 1812 and 1814, the United States and England again fought about land and trade. The United States won the War of 1812. Afterward, the Ojibwe in Michigan, Wisconsin, and Minnesota no longer had dealings with the British. But most of their dealings with the United States harmed them.

The Ojibwe and other tribes signed a treaty in 1825 at Prairie du Chien, Wisconsin.

The Ojibwe signed many treaties with the United States government between 1807 and 1867. Ojibwe leaders such as Hole-in-the-Day bargained in good faith. They thought if they gave up something, they would receive something in return. Many Ojibwe gave up millions of acres of land and agreed to live on reservations. In exchange, the United States promised to give the Ojibwe food, tools, and other goods every year. It promised money for a number of years. The government also allowed the Ojibwe to continue hunting and fishing on their traditional lands. These promises were broken many times.

Ojibwe men traveled to Washington, D.C., to sign a treaty.

A Seth Eastman painting of Ojibwe homes.

Sometimes, as during the Wisconsin Death March, the promises were broken through government trickery. At other times, the terms of a treaty gave little of worth to the Ojibwe. In 1854, Chief Feather's End spoke bitterly about the poor bargain his people had been forced to make in one treaty. He said, "I swallowed the words of the treaty down my throat, and they have not yet had time to blister my breast." By 1867, another Ojibwe leader, White Fisher, did not trust any treaty the government offered. White Fisher said, "I am afraid … that you are making, or doing business in the dark corner, and throwing something in our faces that we cannot see."

In fact, these treaties permitted the settlers to take some Ojibwe land. Mining and lumber companies wanted and took other parts of Ojibwe territory. In 1887, the government passed the Dawes General Allotment Act. This law guaranteed each Ojibwe 160 acres (64 hectares) of reservation land, but it made the rest of the reservation land available for purchase by settlers or companies. This new law was another way in which treaty promises were not kept.

A baby rides in a canoe strapped into a cradleboard as Ojibwe women gather wild rice in 1885.

STRUGGLING FOR RIGHTS

Many missionaries and government officials did not respect native traditions. They believed Ojibwe children should learn the white man's ways. These children were forced to leave their families and live in faraway schools. They were not allowed to speak their own language. Sometimes, children were even given new names. As one Ojibwe remarked, "The white man does

Boys chop wood at an Indian boarding school in 1900.

not scalp the head, but he poisons the heart." This system continued into the 20th century.

Ojibwe also struggled for their promised rights to hunt, gather, and fish in traditional ways. In the 1920s and 1930s, local officials arrested some Ojibwe for these activities even though they were on reservations and other traditional lands.

Yet positive changes also took place. In 1934, the Indian Reorganization Act became a national law. It recognized the rights of tribes to govern themselves. In 1978, the Religious Freedom Act guaranteed the rights of native peoples to practice their religions.

The loss of land and personal rights suffered by native peoples came to national attention through the American Indian Movement (AIM). This organization—with many Ojibwe members including Dennis Banks, Russell Means, and Leonard Peltier—was founded to work for equal rights and improved living conditions

Civil rights leader Ralph Abernathy (left) joined AIM leaders Russell Means and Dennis Banks at Wounded Knee, South Dakota, in March 1973.

for native people. In 1973, AIM members and other Indians took over the South Dakota village of Wounded Knee in a standoff with the Federal Bureau of Investigation (FBI). The AIM protest took place on the site of an 1890 massacre of 300 Sioux by U.S. Cavalry soldiers. The 1973 takeover ended with the surrender of the protesters, but it brought worldwide attention to the problems of native people.

THE OJIBWE TODAY

Woodlands Ojibwe in the United States have strong tribal governments that help them achieve many goals. In Minnesota, Ojibwe on six of the seven reservations have come together as the Minnesota Chippewa Tribe. Its officials are elected by more than 40,000 tribal members. The Ojibwe of Red Lake Reservation in northwestern

High school students ice fish on the Lac Courte Oreilles reservation in Wisconsin.

37

Minnesota have their own tribal government. In Wisconsin and Michigan, individual tribes have their own elected governments, too.

Tribal governments work to try to create helpful laws. In the 1980s, these included state laws that allowed gambling establishments called casinos on reservations. The money produced by tribal casinos benefits each tribal member. It has also helped Ojibwe build schools and hospitals and start businesses on their reservations. In cities, other Ojibwe groups and individuals work to help themselves and protect traditional ways.

Winona LaDuke, a member of Minnesota's White Earth band, is one well-known Ojibwe who speaks for her

Winona LaDuke founded a group to buy back original White Earth land in Minnesota.

people and related causes. In 1996 and 2000, she joined presidential candidate Ralph Nader as his vice presidential running mate on the Green Party ticket.

In October 2000, on the 150th anniversary of the Wisconsin Death March, representatives from many Ojibwe tribes began building a monument at Sandy Lake, Minnesota. It honors the Ojibwe who died there and during the long march homeward. In memory of their brave ancestors, Ojibwe also began a three-day, 150-mile (240 km) run on December 2, 2000. It started with special ceremonies at the Sandy Lake monument.

A relay run from Sandy Lake to Madeline Island honored Ojibwe who died on the Wisconsin Death March.

The Ojibwe are part of modern society, yet their traditions remain very important to most of them. They are proud that their language is now taught in schools on and off the reservation. Ojibwe happily gather at many powwows, where they celebrate and share their traditions. People of all ages enjoy the dancing, singing, and drumming at these events. Today, when it is time to fish, gather mahnomin, or tap maple sap, Ojibwe in cities often return to their reservations. They enjoy continuing these traditions with family and friends.

A dancer at an Ojibwe powwow

On and off the reservation, some Ojibwe struggle with health problems or need jobs. There are still legal arguments with the government about Ojibwe rights to hunt and fish. There are also questions about how agricultural

Men harvest wild rice on the Leech Lake Reservation.

research may affect the Ojibwe's sacred food, wild rice. The Ojibwe, though, are hopeful about the future. They believe in their own efforts. They see other people recognizing the wisdom in traditional Ojibwe concern for the earth and future generations.

41

GLOSSARY

allies—people or countries who agree to help each other in times of trouble

clan—a group of people related by blood or marriage

fasted—went without food

immunity—the ability of the body to resist a disease

marten—a small animal like a weasel

nomads—people who travel from place to place to hunt and gather food

pictographs—writing that uses pictures to represent ideas

prophecy—a view of the future that may come from God

provinces—divisions of some countries; Canada has 10 provinces and three territories

reservations—large areas of land set aside for Native Americans; in Canada, reservations are called reserves

sweat lodges—buildings in which heat causes the occupants to perspire, to purify the body and spirit

DID YOU KNOW?

- The word *Ojibwe* is also spelled Ojibwa and Ojibway.

- The name *Ojibwe* may come from the Ojibwe word for "puckered." The Ojibwe used an unusual style of puckered stitches to sew their moccasins. Another source for this name might be the Ojibwe word for "written records."

- The English words *moose* and *moccasin* come from the Ojibwe language.

- The combined population of all the Ojibwe living in the United States and Canada today is more than 200,000 people.

- Wild rice is not really rice. It is a kind of grain that grows on top of long grass.

- The Ojibwe are one of the native peoples who first played the outdoor sport now called lacrosse.

- Charles Albert Bender, an Ojibwe from Minnesota, was a professional baseball player. In 1953, he was elected to the Baseball Hall of Fame.

IMPORTANT DATES

Timeline

900	Ancestors of the Ojibwe living on the Eastern seaboard begin to move west.
1400	Ancestors of the Ojibwe arrive in the Midwest; by 1545, they have spread throughout Wisconsin and Minnesota.
1615	French explorers and fur traders meet the Ojibwe and neighboring tribes.
1630	Ojibwe and other native peoples war with each other over land; these conflicts last for more than 130 years.
1850	Wisconsin Death March takes place.
1867	Last of many treaties in which the Ojibwe give up land and agree to live on reservations.
1887	The Dawes General Allotment Act becomes law; it decreases native lands.
2000	On the 150th anniversary of the Wisconsin Death March, the Ojibwe honor their dead with a monument in Sandy Lake and a 150-mile (240 kilometer) run.

Important People

Dennis Banks (1937–)
One of the Ojibwe founders of the American Indian Movement

Hole-in-the-Day (1825–1868)
Important Ojibwe chief of the 19th century

Winona LaDuke (1959–)
Modern leader of the Ojibwe people who has also been active in politics

Russell Means (1939–)
One of the Ojibwe spokesmen of the American Indian Movement;
Means has also worked in the film industry, appearing in The Last of
the Mohicans *and providing the voice of Powhatan in* Pocahontas

Leonard Peltier (1944–)
Prominent Ojibwe member of the American Indian Movement; he is a
controversial person who is now in prison convicted–unfairly, some
people say–of murder during the takeover at Wounded Knee in 1973

William Warren (1825–1853)
Historian and government worker whose mother was Ojibwe,
he listened to elders and wrote a history of the Ojibwe in English
in 1852; the book was published in 1885

WANT TO KNOW MORE?

At the Library

Bial, Raymond. *The Ojibwe*. New York: Marshall Cavendish, 2000.

DeAngelis, Therese. *The Ojibwa: Wild Rice Gatherers*. Mankato, Minn.: Blue Earth Books, 2003.

Erdrich, Louise. *The Birchbark House*. New York: Hyperion, 2002.

Van Laan, Nancy. *Shingebiss: An Ojibwe Legend*. Boston: Houghton Mifflin, 1997.

On the Web

For more information on the *Ojibwe,* use FactHound to track down Web sites related to this book.

1. Go to *www.facthound.com*

2. Type in a search word related to this book or this book ID: 0756508436.

3. Click on the *Fetch It* button.

Your trusty FactHound will fetch the best Web sites for you!

On the Road

Grand Portage National Monument

315 S. Broadway

Grand Marais, MN 55604-0668

218/387-2788

Visit this U.S. government historic site located within the Grand Portage Indian reservation to see how Ojibwe and fur traders lived in the late 1700s

National Museum of the American Indian

Fourth Street and Independence Avenue Southwest

Washington, DC 20560

202/287-2020

Visit this Smithsonian Institution museum to learn more about the Ojibwe and other native peoples

Look for more We the People books about this era:

The Alamo

The Arapaho and Their History

The Battle of the Little Bighorn

The Buffalo Soldiers

The California Gold Rush

The Chumash and Their History

The Creek and Their History

The Erie Canal

Great Women of the Old West

The Lewis and Clark Expedition

The Louisiana Purchase

The Mexican War

The Oregon Trail

The Pony Express

The Powhatan and Their History

The Santa Fe Trail

The Transcontinental Railroad

The Trail of Tears

The Wampanoag and Their History

The War of 1812

A complete list of We the People titles is available on our Web site:
www.compasspointbooks.com

INDEX

About the Author

Natalie M. Rosinsky writes about history, social studies, economics, science, and other fun things. One of her two cats usually sits on her computer as she works in Mankato, Minnesota. Natalie earned graduate degrees from the University of Wisconsin and has been a high school and college teacher.